Through Irish Eyes

A VISUAL COMPANION TO Angela McCourt's Ireland

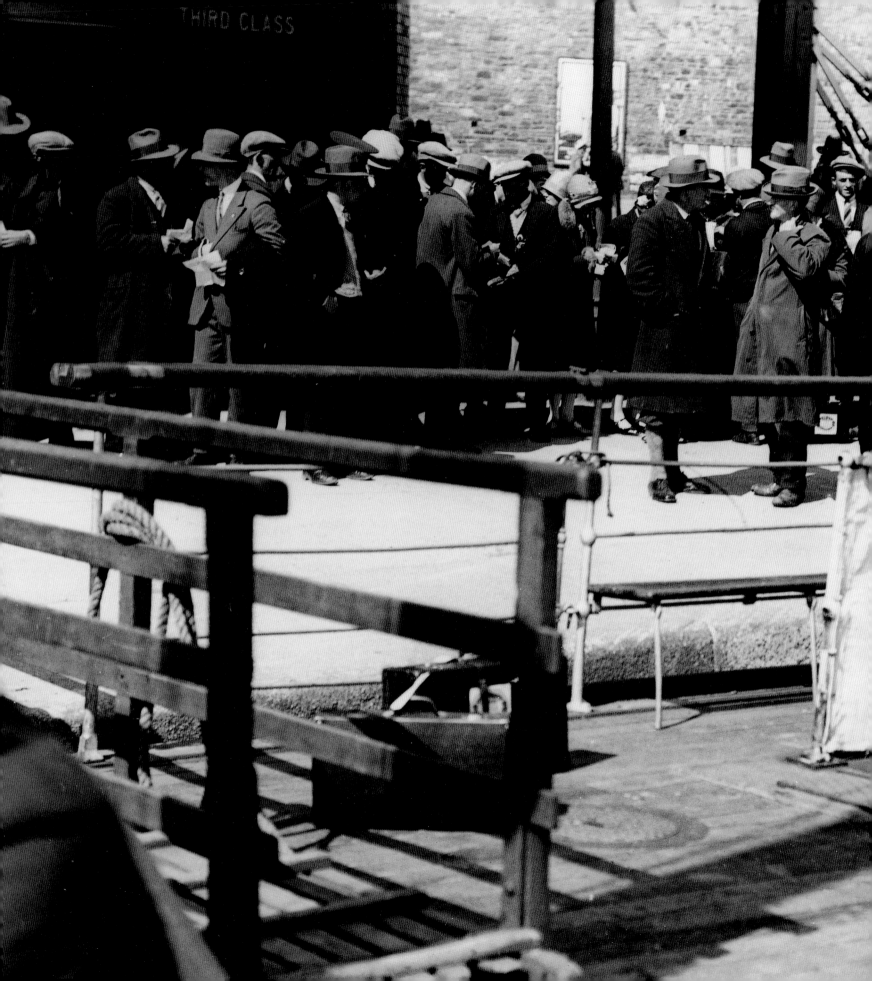

Through Irish Eyes

A VISUAL COMPANION TO Angela McCourt's Ireland

FOREWORD BY

Malachy McCourt

Glitterati
INCORPORATED

New York | London

This edition published in 2013 by

Glitterati Incorporated
New York – London

New York Office:
322 West 57th Street #19T
New York, NY10019
Telephone: 212 362 9119

London Office:
1 Rona Road
London NW3 2HY
Tel/Fax +44 (0) 207 267 9739

www.GlitteratiIncorporated.com — media@GlitteratiIncorporated.com for inquiries

Library of Congress Cataloging-in-Publication data is available from the publisher

Edited, designed and produced by Haldane Mason Ltd, London
Pictures and text compiled by David Pritchard
Art Director: Ron Samuel
Editorial Director: Christopher Fagg
Editor: David Ross
Picture Research: David Pritchard
Design: Zoë Mellors

Hardcover edition ISBN 13: 978-0-9851696-7-1
Printed in China
10 9 8 7 6 5 4 3 2 1

Contents

Foreword

"Limerick—a labyrinth of swarming poverty and squalid commerce as was never seen—no not in St. Giles where the Jews and the Irish display their genius for dirt."

—**William Makepeace Thackeray,** *An Irish Scrapbook of 1842*

I didn't want to write a foreword to this or any other picture prose book about the Ireland of my youth. Why? Because before I saw what it was going to be about, I assumed it was going to be another tooral ooral addie depiction of happy milkmaids and leaping farm laborers doing the chaste Walls of Ennis, as choreographed by Holy Mother Church and Daddy DeValera, supervised by His Reverence the parish priest.

It would, I thought, show an Ireland that exists only in the minds of the Shure Begorrah Brigades that pollute the papers and indeed all the media around the green ghetto days surrounding the feast of St. Patrick—the intruder who did more to ruin than any Brit. But that was before I saw and read *Through Irish Eyes*.

To my surprised delight, the book is honest and it is deserving of wide circulation among all of us who suffered poverty, cruelty, and deprivation—be it under the Turks in Armenia, the knout of the Cossacks in Tsarist Russia, or the famines of India and Ireland under benevolent British Raj rule.

Oh yes, I was surprised too at the welter of savage emotion that surged through my mind, and especially at the description of Mr. Kane of Dispensary fame who handed out the miserable pittance to my mother and other destitute women. It was often we children stood in the shelter of her coat while he counted out the thirteen shillings and six pence. Before handing the coins of the realm, he would bellow vile insults, accusations of dishonesty for receiving money under false pretenses. Yet here that vicious bully is described by some Limerick scribe as a man of kindness, compassion who abhorred poor people because he felt so deeply about their misfortunate lot in life. Thanks be to Jesus he didn't feel any deeper or he'd have us all shot to put us out of our misery.

Hurrah for revolution and more cannon-shot!
A beggar upon horseback lashes a beggar on foot.
Hurrah for revolution and cannon come again!
The beggars have changed places, but the lash goes on.

—**W. B. Yeats,** *The Great Day*

There will be some on this side of the Atlantic who will sigh and say, "Ain't it quaint" and plan a trip to the "old sod" in search of slums and slummery and the charming characters who can spout poetic sayings and colorful prose at the appearance of a pint. The lanes are gone, the people are not, and the inquiring visitor may be told that what is pictured and prosed in *Through Irish Eyes* never existed, that those in the life of *Angela's Ashes* are imagination figments.

Herein captured for all time in pictures are the women, the men, the children, not of the lowest order, but of no order, for they came unbidden. The children smile (it's a camera for God's sake) and the enslaved women at the sewing machines in the clothing factory sweat shop try to look suitably grateful and respectful (Jesus, Bridgid, you never know who might look at a picture and spot sullen rebellion. Then where would you be, out on your arse for there's plenty more wanting your job).

So I raged and wept and cursed at the savages, domestic and foreign, who visited such cruelty on a graceful, generous people, but then allowed the peace and serenity to fill my soul again because I am with hope and faith that those bestial days are done. That this wonderful work *Through Irish Eyes* will always be the classic and classical reminder that the poor are always with us somewhere, and it's been a long wait for the meek to inherit the earth. Look at this book carefully and keep it close, lest we and our children and their children forget.

> Parnell came down the road, he said to a cheering man:
> "Ireland should get her freedom and you still break stone."
> —**W. B. Yeats,** *Parnell*

—Malachy McCourt
New York, May 1998

Irish children playing in the street, 1930s.

The Long Streets of Brooklyn

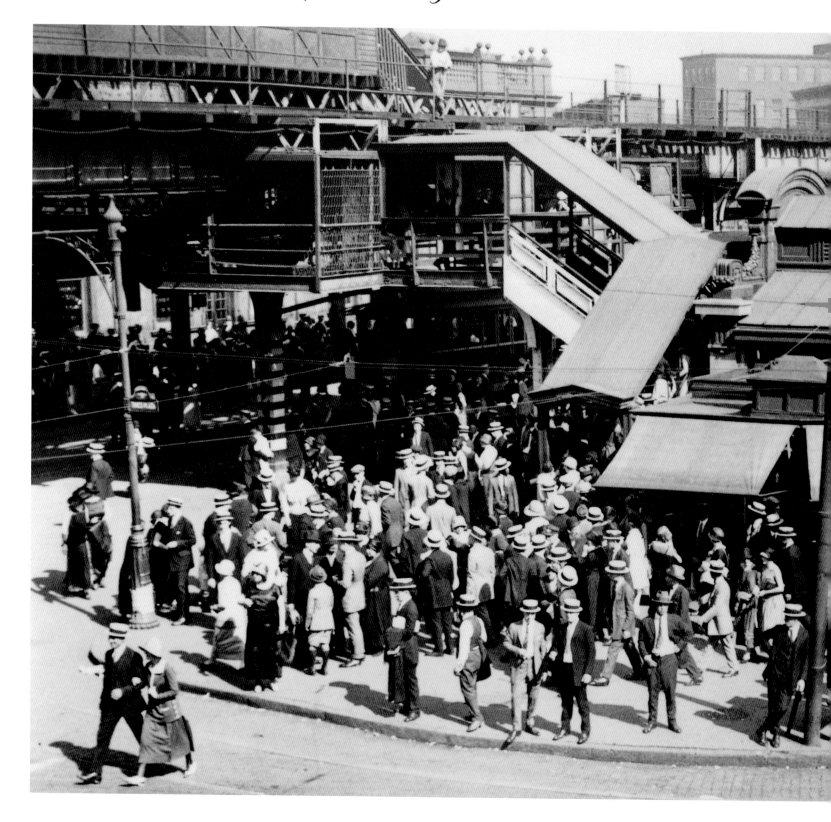

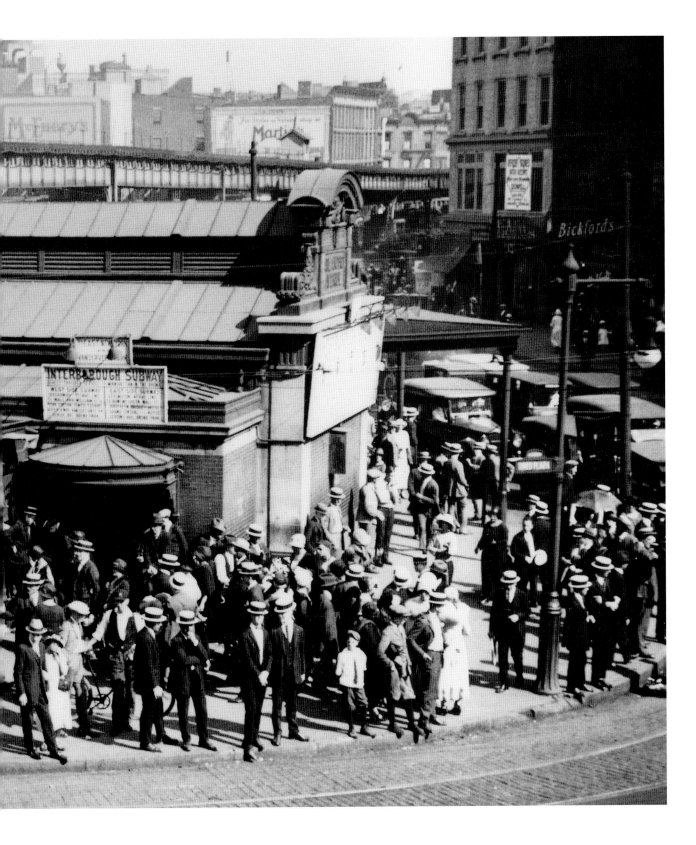

The subway kiosk at Atlantic Avenue, Brooklyn, circa 1930. New York was the crucible of Irish America, where Frank McCourt and his brother Malachy were born, and from where they were taken to Ireland.

. . . And So to Limerick

O'Connell Street, Limerick, in the 1930s.

O'Connell Street is still Limerick's main shopping street, and some of the same names may still be seen above the doors. Limerick was then, and still is, Ireland's third city, next in size after Dublin and Cork, and capital of a great region in the West. A seaport and market town, its main industries were a cement works and a flour mill. Like all Irish towns in the still-formative years of independence, its population included those who were relatively well-off, or securely employed—including policemen, civil servants and teachers. But there was not enough work available to ensure employment for everyone. It was a buyer's market for labor, and women workers especially were miserably paid. Those without work had few resources. Just off the city center, Limerick's Lanes and Quays were the parts of the city where the least-paid and the unemployed congregated—but even here there were rents to be paid.

However modern the main roads of 1930s Limerick, Cork and Dublin, with their automobiles and electric street-lighting, the poorer back-streets were dilapidated slums.

I recall when I started in strange lands to roam,
Sure 'tis little I thought how I'd miss me ould home
Miss the old folks, the village, the valley so green,
And the road by the river that flows through Raheen.

–Anonymous, quoted in *Angela's Ashes*

Hunt's Lane, off Parnell Street, Limerick, 1933.

"After you get out of the Main Street the handsome part of the town is at an end, and you suddenly find yourself in such a labyrinth of busy swarming poverty and squalid commerce as never was seen—no not in Saint Giles's where Jew and Irishman side by side exhibit their genius for dirt. Here every house was almost half a ruin, and swarming with people; in the cellars you looked down and saw a barrel of herrings which a merchant was dispensing; or a sack of meat, which a poor dirty woman sold to people dirtier and poorer than herself; above was a tinman or shoemaker or other craftsman, his battered ensign at the door and his small wares peeping through the cracked panes of his shop."

William Makepeace Thackeray,
An Irish Scrapbook of 1842

Nothing Left but the Dispensary

NOT LESSENED.

Needs of the Poor

A quarterly general meeting of the Limerick Conferences of the Society of St. Vincent de Paul was held at Ozanam House on Sunday last, his Lordship the Bishop, Most Rev. Dr. Keane, presiding. The attendance included Rev. Dr. Cowper, Adm., St. Michael's, and Rev. J. S. Cates, S.J., Crescent College.

There were now so many works of relief for the poor, said his Lordship, that he had thought that the demands on their Society would have been lessened, but he found that was not so. They were as big as they had been in late years, if not greater, and their balance-sheet submitted to the meeting showed that the big reserve they had gathered a couple of years ago had been exhausted, and that they were now meeting their relief bills through the varying sums which had been coming into them, and through the realisation of some of their trusts. To carry on their commendable work of charity funds would always be needed, and he was sure responses to their appeals would always be forthcoming. He thanked the members for all they were doing. It was a time of hardship for all, but especially for the poor, when not only were commodities so much dearer, but it was in many cases impossible to procure the necessaries of life. They should ever be actuated by the spirit of Frederick Ozanam, their founder, finding their delight in serving the poor and assisting them how and when possible. Considering their own needs in a spirit of patience and forbearance, he would remind them of the dire necessities and stark starvation prevailing in other countries, and he would recommend to the prayers of the people the homes of the people on the Continent, who are suffering so much in privations and disasters, and where hundreds were dying from sheer want owing to the supplies of the necessaries of life having been suspended. The Irish Red Cross were doing good work in their charitable endeavours in even a little way alleviating the lot of these people. It was hard to see —perhaps not possible to see—an ending to the war, and intelligent foresight is needed in planning for our own necessities. The fact that fertilisers are scarce is a handicap to those who toil to produce our food, but shortages and difficulties in procuring necessaries are now commonplaces. He urged the members to keep on at their good work, and he hoped that the coming of summer would lessen the hardships on the poor.

BALANCE SHEET.

His Lordship had been speaking to the reports from the various Conferences which had been submitted at the meeting. The balance-sheet had shown that in relief in kind the Society had during the past twelve months expended in Limerick the sum of £2,040, and close on £600 on boots and clothing. The expenditure had been greater than the income, and it was pointed out that the Boot Scheme recently started in the city had alleviated to a great extent the problem confronting the Society of providing boots for poor families. As it has been, both in the matter of boots and bedding and clothing, the Society have only been able to supply a quota of the many applications made to them, and these to the more deserving applicants or the larger families, and it is a source of satisfaction that these have been supplemented by the recently formed scheme for supplying boots to the school-going children of the poor, just as in the matter of fuel the Muintir na Tire organisation came to the help of the Society earlier.

On February 29, 1944, the Limerick Chronicle *reported a quarterly general meeting of the Society of St. Vincent de Paul, for many years the major provider of charitable relief to the poor of Ireland. Addressing the meeting, Bishop Keane pointed out that the needs of the poor remained as great as ever.*

Thus, more than forty years into the twentieth century, the endemic poverty of Ireland remained as stark an issue as it had to the concerned Victorians of the nineteenth. Poverty in turn fueled successive waves of emigration to Canada, the U.S.A. and Australia, as well as to the U.K., until there were more people of direct Irish descent living out of the island of Ireland than existed in North and South together. Only over the last twenty years, with a resurgent Irish economy benefiting from transatlantic investment and membership of the European Community, have the people of Ireland been able to feel that the specters of poverty, economic depression and wide-scale unemployment have been banished from the Irish experience.

"There were no social-welfare handouts as we know them today, except for the niggardly mites handed out to the very poor at the city dispensary by the relieving officer. This unenviable office was held for many years by Tom Kane, a native of Parteen. Tom was a gentle giant of well over six feet, and weighed about seventeen stone or thereabouts. He had a powerful bellowing voice that could be heard at the off side of Gerald Griffin Street as he used his only weapons against the crowd of pitifully plaintive suppliants who gathered around his office in the drab Dickensian building. His name was a bye-word in Limerick for more than thirty years. People in extreme poverty were advised by others to 'go to Kane.' It was just like sending them to the devil. Most of those who had to endure the humiliation of the Dispensary had nothing good to say of Tom. To some he was a 'dog,' to others a tyrant and a savage. In reality he was kind and considerate and felt compassion for those at whom he roared in order to convince them that he had only a small sum of money to distribute amongst far too many.

"He was a splendid character who had to endure the weekly insults of the poor people who believed him to be a fairy godfather who was keeping all the money for himself. The weekly budget was so small that the average sum payable to families was about half a crown (twenty cents). It was known that Tom's compassion was often so stirred at the sight of a disappointed applicant, when the last shilling had been doled out, that he gave some assistance out of his own pocket."

Kevin Hannon, *Old Limerick Journal* 16

"Is there outside Hell anything approaching the conditions under which the poor are forced to live in 17 Jones's Row? White's Lane is the same. Pump Lane, Dixon's Lane, Hell's Lane, Walshe's Lane, Punche's Lane, Upper Carey's Road and Roxboro Road all bereft of sanitary convenience. Boys, girls, men and women eat, drink, sleep and wash in these. Rents are squeezed from the poor of these houses by the owners. It is against the laws of God to leave these helpless beings any longer in chains."

W. J. L., article in the broadsheet *The Bottom Dog,* **1918**

From the Limerick Chronicle,
February 29, 1944.

"But If at Last our Colour Should Be Torn from Ireland's Heart"

The Treaty Stone, in its former location at Sarsfield Bridge, Limerick.

Limerick and its region have played a vigorous part in Ireland's stormy history. The city was once entirely walled, and within it there is a Norman castle, "King John's Castle." There are numerous other castles in the surrounding area, including the ruined Carrigogunnell and the now fully restored Bunratty, visited by many thousands each year. But Limerick's proudest time was the great siege endured in the seventeenth century, under the leadership of Patrick Sarsfield.

"The memory of Limerick that I, and I suppose everyone, takes away is that of a fine bridge over the Shannon which at this point is a wide and splendid river. At one end of this bridge rise the massive rounded towers of an ancient castle; at the other end is one of the sights of Ireland: a big, rough boulder now much chipped by souvenir hunters which stands mounted on a plinth. This is the famous 'Treaty Stone'. . . . When a man stands at the Treaty Stone of Limerick he remembers a hero whom any nation would be proud to honour: Patrick Sarsfield. . . . It was on the large slab of stone at the bridgehead that Patrick Sarsfield signed the famous treaty of Limerick (in 1690). The Irish were by this treaty to enjoy full civil and religious liberty and all Irish soldiers who had fought for King James were to be given a free passage to France. . . . They had no sooner left the shores of Ireland than the treaty was violated."

—H. V. Morton, *In Search of Ireland*

St. Patrick's Day

"But if at last our colour should be torn from Ireland's heart,
    Her sons, with shame and sorrow, from the dear ould isle will part;
I've heard a whisper of a land that lies beyond the sea,
    Where rich and poor stand equal in the light of freedom's day.
Ah! Erin! Must we leave you, driven by a tyrant's hand?
    Must we seek a mother's blessing from a strange and distant land?
Where the cruel cross of England shall never more be seen,
    And where, please God, we'll live and die, still wearin' o' the green!"

                                        —**Anonymous, nineteenth century**

15

Decrepit as they often were, the back streets of Irish towns and cities were never short of interest and incident. The elements of these photographs make an intriguing composition: the calling man, the hooded nuns, the dog, the children—and the inevitable person watching it all from a window.

The St. Vincent de Paul Society Wants to Know When She'll Stop Asking for Charity

The Society of Saint Vincent de Paul played an important role in sustaining the poor through charitable activities. Jobs were scarce and even the low-paid garment workers in the photograph opposite might have found it hard to get by. However, the Society's attitude to poor families like the McCourts was more concerned with the health of souls than of bodies.

"The following suggestions may be helpful for Social Workers on visitation of homes where there are cases of sickness.

1. Tactfully encourage cleanliness and fresh air in the room. See that they have the help of sacred representations, Crucifix (blessed with the indulgence for the hour of death), images of Our Lady and the Saints.

2. Remind the friends of the sick person to assist them if necessary in making Acts of Faith, Hope and Charity, of resignation to God's Will and acts of contrition or sorrow for their sins. But they should not be wearied with long prayers; short fervent aspirations and offerings of their pain and weariness will be best."

The Saint Vincent de Paul Social Workers' Handbook, 1942

Workers in a Limerick garment factory, circa 1930

We Might As Well Have a Pint Before We Go, Joe

"As is well known there is a large consumption of porter and whiskey amongst the labouring classes. In many cases an undue proportion of their earnings is spent on these beverages, with consequent deprivations of home comforts and even necessaries.

"The workman is blamed for visiting the public-house, but it is to him what the club is to the rich man. His home is rarely a comfortable one, and in winter the bright light, the warm fire and the gaiety of the public-house are attractions which he finds difficult to resist. If he spends a reasonable proportion of his earnings in the public-house is he more to be condemned than the prosperous shop-keeper or professional man who drinks expensive wine at the club or restaurant, spends hours playing billiards or cards and amuses himself in other expensive ways? At the same time it cannot be denied that there is much intemperance amongst the working classes and that the women, who were formerly rarely seen intoxicated, are now frequently to be observed in that state. The publicans themselves are averse to drunkards. Their best customers are the men who spend a moderate proportion of their wages in drink, for the drunkards lose their situations."

Sir Charles Cameron, *How the Poor Live,* 1904

"Coughs and Colds Are Prevalent"

This warning headline to a classified ad in a 1943 edition of the Limerick Chronicle *enjoined readers: "Be sure to ask for Emby's Essence of Benzoin by name (registered) and avoid substitutes. Emby's warms up chest, cuts away phlegm and has an unexcelled reputation for doing what it says. IT CURES COUGHS." This good news appeared next to a large ad for the movie* Something to Shout About, *starring Don Ameche and Janet Blair. Yet the reality for the poor populations of cities like Limerick, Cork and Dublin was grimmer: diseases such as T.B. and diptheria continued to take their toll in the 1930s as they had at the turn of the century.*

Classified ad from the
Limerick Chronicle in 1943.

> tions carefully executed.
> COUGHS AND COLDS are prevalent. Be sure to ask for **Emby's Essence of Benzoin** by name (registered) and avoid substitutes. Emby's warms up chest, cuts away phlegm, and has an unexcelled reputation for doing what it says. IT CURES COUGHS. Sold by all chemists. Manufactured by WIDDESS, Chemist, Roche's Street. 1/6 and 2/6 per bottle. Special Children's Essence, 1/3.
> O'DONOVAN'S for Best Quality Anthracite and Turf; also Hardwood Blocks.—Phone 250.

Guidelines for the treatment of T.B. patients in Ireland, published in the early 1900s.

Women's National Health Association of Ireland.

RULES FOR CONSUMPTIVE PATIENTS.

Consumption is a catching disease. It may pass from person to person.

The chief source of infection is to be found in the phlegm of the consumptive. The great danger lies in the drying of the spits, and the blowing about of the dried infectious material.

The spread of consumption can be largely prevented.

When at home, the patient should spit into a jar or cup containing some fluid.

The vessel should be changed once in twelve hours, or oftener. It should be cleansed by being filled up with *boiling* water. The combined contents should be poured down the w.c. The vessel should then be washed with *boiling* water.

When the patient is out of doors, he should carry a pocket flask. The flask should be used and cleansed like the jar. The patient should never spit in the streets, or on floors.

The phlegm should on no account be swallowed.

Consumptive mothers should not suckle.

Patients with advanced disease should have special table utensils if possible.

Rooms which have been occupied by a consumptive patient should, before occupation by someone else, be carefully disinfected, as after any other infectious disease.

FRESH AIR is *the food of the lungs.* Therefore see that the lungs are not starved.

A.—By Day.—The patient should occupy as airy a room as possible. *The window should be freely open.* When able the patient should be out of doors during the day. He must *avoid over-effort* and chill.

B.—By Night.—He should sleep alone. The bedroom should be large and airy. The *window should be kept freely open* in all weathers.

Irish pub, 1930s.

It's a Long Way to the Dock Road

Limerick did considerable seaborne trade. Large ocean-going ships could berth by the flour mills to unload grain. Smaller coasting vessels brought coal from Wales, and there were regular cargo lines to other Irish ports and to Liverpool. Coal boats were unloaded at the docks, and the coal carts usually dropped a few lumps as they jolted their way along to the yards. In winter, children were sent with old perambulators and sacks to gather such coal as they could find in the Dock Road.

A panoramic view of the city seen from Limerick Docks in the 1930s. The view looks up the Shannon to the Sarsfield Bridge. The Quays and the Lanes of Limerick were situated in the area of the top right-hand quarter of the photograph.

Limerick Landmarks

Wealth, or the lack of it, played a part in people's perception of their own city. For the well-off, the big shops, the hotels, the nicer houses, might first come to mind. For the poor, it was the places where entrance was free: churches, hospitals, the library, the park. Such buildings often had a stern and forbidding appearance—their severe style served to remind the people that nothing should be taken for granted. They might be open to all, but they were still the abodes of authority. And their doors could be shut against those who were not seen to be fit to enter.

St. John's Hospital, Limerick

The Library.

St. John's Hospital.

*The Franciscan Church, where
Frankie lit a candle to get out of class.*

"We'll go back to St. Joseph's and pray
that from now on everyone in Mickey
Spellacy's family will die in the middle of
the summer . . ."

—**Frank McCourt,** *Angela's Ashes*

St. Joseph's Church.

The Open Air

The ruined Norman castle of Carrigogunnell, Limerick, as it looked in the 1930s. This ancient castle, the remains of which still stand outside the city, overlooking the River Shannon, was young Frank McCourt's favorite place of escape.

Children's party at the open-air swimming pool at Corbally, near Limerick.

The People's Park.

"The People's Park was our playground; it was a wonderland all of its own. We played at sports or just enjoyed ourselves. Vandalism was unheard of. Our biggest crime was 'skinning' orchards: the best one was at the Christian Brothers School. The Brothers grew the biggest apples, which we called turnips."

Paul Malone,
"Memories of Picquet Lane,"
Old Limerick Journal 16

Limerick was a small city. Within its limits was the People's Park, a favorite strolling area and children's playground. But even a child could walk right out of the town and into the country and find himself among fields where cows and sheep were grazing. In the 1930s and 1940s there was little traffic, and much of it was horse-drawn. It was a safe environment, and a source of adventure. On fine days there was also the open-air swimming pool, far safer than the swift and treacherous river.

Out to the Country

Road bowling, in which a ball is hurled great distances along country roads, was a popular rural sport.

Desmond Castle, in Adare near Limerick, was long the seat of the Fitzgerald family. The oldest ruins date from the thirteenth century.

Thomond Bridge and King John's Castle, Limerick. A horse and cart could take you out to the country along the quiet roads of 1930s Ireland.

How the Poor Lived

The 1911 Census of Ireland offers a rare glimpse into the lives of the inhabitants of the Limerick Lanes. The Harrigans of Barrack Lane were a typical Roman Catholic laboring family of the area, existing on the edge of poverty in uncomfortable and crowded conditions. At the time of the census Stephen and Elizabeth Harrigan had been married for twenty years and were living in a two-room house with their eight children. Only sixteen on her wedding day, Elizabeth had borne twelve children not counting miscarriages, four of whom were already dead, most likely in infancy. Patrick, her oldest child, was nineteen and worked on the docks with his father; Angelica, her youngest child, was only three years old. Seventeen-year-old Mary Harrigan was employed as a seamstress, probably in one of Limerick's garment factories, while the remaining children were still in school.

On the form, Elizabeth states her place of birth as Canada. Her parents may have been returned immigrants, but it is also possible that her father was a soldier in the adjacent army barracks. She could also read and write, unlike her illiterate husband.

Poor Irish children, photographed in the early years of the century.

The Lanes

The conditions under which the McCourts lived in Roden Lane were by no means unusual. In 1942, when the Limerick Corporation was deciding whether or not to demolish a large section of lanes around Carey's Road, a house-to-house survey was carried out. Almost all the dwellings were found to be in a state of disrepair, with varying degrees of structural damage. In many houses the floors were at a lower level than the street, leaving them susceptible to dampness and flooding. The Lanes were also grossly overcrowded, with families of up to twelve people living in tiny two-room houses.

Arthur's Mews, Limerick, photographed in the 1930s.

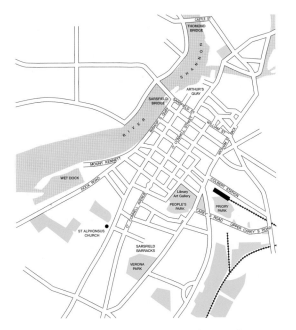

Above: A map of Limerick today, showing the location of the old Lanes area, now demolished.
Below: The 1942 city council report on dwellings in the Lanes detailed the dilapadation, over-occupancy and primitive amenities of the area.

Plan of the Limerick Lanes in 1942, prior to their clearance by the city council. The map reveals the huddled intimacy of the little streets and alleys, suggesting why they were such hotbeds of diseases like typhoid, diphtheria and consumption.

Existence of Fireplace	No. of Occupants	Width from rere to rere of Houses	Water Supply	Sanitary Arrangements	GENERAL OBSERVATIONS
F. P. ---- ----	6	19' 0"	Tap	None	Walls ad kitchen damp, rain down on ceiling lime mortar floor in bad repair. Bedroom walls damp and rain down on ceiling. Rain down in a tic and floor in bad repair No yard drainage or W.C. Rere wall unplastered. No eaves gutters on front or back of house and roof in very bad repair.
F. P. ---- ----	6	19' 0"	Tap	None	Walls of kitchen and bedroom damp. Attic not used . No yard drainage or W. C. No eaves gutters on front or back of house and back wall unplastered externally. Roof in bad repair.
F. P. ---- ----	5	20' 0"	Tap	None	Walls of kitchen and bedroom damp, rain down on kitchen ceiling and bedroom floor in bad repair. Attic not used. Annexe very damp. No yard drainage or W.C. No eaves gutters on front or back of house and back wall unplastered externally.
F. P. ---- ---- ----	5	20' 0"	Tap	None	Kitchen floor 4" below lane and 4" below yard level Lime mortar floor in bad repair, walls damp and in very bad repair. Bedroom walls damp. Rain down on Attic ceiling and walls damp. Sides and roof of annexe leaking. No yard drainage or W.C. Rere wall unplastered externally and front poorly plastered.
	5	20' 0"	Tap	None	Kitchen floor, walls and ceiling in bad rep walls and ceiling in bedroom in bad repair Rain down in attic and walls in very bad W.C. or yard drainage. No eaves gut back of house and back and front

"And there were many houses full of children in those days, as women were encouraged to have children, irrespective of the means of providing for them. In the poorer districts families were crowded into earthen-floored cabins having only one or two apartments, or huddled in the garrets of cottered houses. There was incredible squalor and overcrowding with all its attendant disease and a high mortality rate among children. I remember seeing two boys go with a bucket into the street to collect mud for the purpose of repairing a pot-hole in their bedroom floor."

—Kevin Hannon, "In My Own Time,"
Old Limerick Journal 16

The Quays

The eighteenth century saw a great surge of new building in Limerick. Fine tall houses of handsome proportions were built along the the bank of the Shannon, with a view of the riverside scene. The Georgian architecture rivaled that of Dublin in distinction if not in extent. But, as happened also in Dublin and Cork, the passage of time brought about a change in the pattern of housing. The merchants and other wealthier inhabitants moved away from the river, further from the city center, and to houses with more in the way of modern facilities. The grand old houses were bought up by landlords and subdivided into tenement flats or single rooms. By the twentieth century, many families were crowded into these buildings, living in conditions of appalling squalor and degradation.

Looking across the Shannon from the Quays, Limerick.

Arthur's Quay.

"A few scattered villas and a brand-new all-electricity house warned me we were approaching Limerick. Past some dull terraces and suddenly we seemed back in the eighteenth century. Only the raw bricks of a Jesuit college warned me that the Crescent we were now entering was not a dream, that I should not be seeing patches and powder on the pavements. Down the long continuous thoroughfare of Patrick and Rutland Street to Charlotte Quay we went, between rows of lovely Georgian houses of dark red brick, built apparently to one pattern. Even the porticoes are uniform. A pair of Ionic pillars above a stately flight of stone steps supports each beautiful fanlight, and with few exceptions the windows with their twelve or sixteen panes remain intact. But the houses themselves are sadly ravaged, glass out of a fanlight here, a broken step there. And when we reached Charlotte Quay I was appalled at the squalor. Swarms of ragged children ran in and out of the great doors, for these palatial houses have now become a hive of tenement houses occupied by the poorest of the poor."

"Round the corner are the Old Custom House with its riverside garden, and other quays, their tall houses all showing the same sad face. And past them flows the strong tide of the Shannon from which the Atlantic breezes blow, fresh and cleansing."

—**Dorothy McCall, "A Visit to Limerick 1938,"** *Old Limerick Journal*

In the Fever Hospital

"I fear that being a patient in any hospital in Ireland calls for two things —holy resignation and an iron constitution."

—**Myles na Gopaleen,**
The Nationalist and Leinster Times

Hospitals were not the cheerful, open places that they are today. Improvements in medical knowledge and patient care, and changes in social attitudes, have brought about a great transformation. But in the 1930s and 1940s they were still authoritarian places. Care was free, but the poor were made to feel that they were being looked after on sufferance. The slightest hint of enjoyment or high spirits was heavily frowned upon. The natural kindness of the nurses was chilled into repression by the inhuman formality of the system. There was another presence in the hospitals too—and that was fear. By the time someone was admitted, it might well be too late. There were many diseases considered incurable. Especially in the tuberculosis wards, many people, old and young, were admitted in the expectation that they would die there. The ever-present fear of death helped to create the chilly, brooding atmosphere that sometimes also seems reflected in the architecture itself.

A nurse was in a hospital
   In the afternoon brightness
And pulses there were throbbing
   Regularly in beds;
She stood before each bedstead
   And stayed a short while counting,
Jotting down the measure
   Syllabling in each wrist;
She syllabled herself at length
   Rhythmically from the ward
And left behind a chorus
   Of pulses keeping time:
It was then the Angelus spread its
   Syllable-scale across lips there
Till Amens died away
   Like whispering in the ward:
But the murmuring continued
   In the monastery of flesh,
The pulses going like monks
   Syllabling their plain-chant.

—**Seán Ó Ríordáin,**
Syllabling,
translated from Gaelic by Patrick Crotty

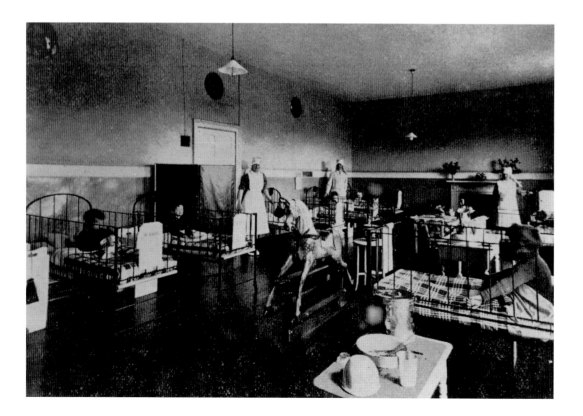

Children's ward, Limerick, 1930s.

A Limerick funeral procession, with horse-drawn hearse.

"Who's Comin' in the Carriage?"

"When I saw her first reclining
Her lips were mov'd in prayer,
And the setting sun was shining
On her loosen'd golden hair.
When our kindly glances met her
Deadly brilliant was her eye;
And she said that she was better,
While we knew that she would die."

—**Richard d'Alton Williams,**
The Dying Girl (extract)

At that time, all funerals had horse-drawn hearses and carriages. There was a mourning coach (somewhat larger than the ordinary carriages) in which relatives of the deceased traveled.

"T.B. was rampant and a lot of families were bereaved. When babies died they were buried quietly in tiny timber boxes. Few people could afford medicine or even a decent funeral."

—**Paul Malone, "Memories of Picquet Lane,"**
Old Limerick Journal 16

Mortuary chapel scene in a Dublin hospital.

Children of the Street

From homes that were intolerably cramped and crowded, the children came out whenever they could to play in the streets. They did not have toys, but they did not lack amusements. Stones, pieces of wood or rope, all could be turned into playthings by dint of imagination.

The windows of the little shops, packed with things they could rarely afford, were a source of endless interest. They played the same games, and chanted the same rhymes, all across the country.

" 'I've a pain in me belly,'
  Says Doctor Kelly.
'Rub it with oil,'
  Says Doctor Boyle.
'A very good cure,'
  Says Doctor Moore."

—Anonymous

Brotherly love.

"In those days the uncluttered streets were the playgrounds of the city. Each district had its own special building or gable-end as a handball alley. Hurling and football were played on the streets. I remember playing foot-ball and 'rounders' in Cathedral Street, where funerals always upset the game, as the best place for the wickets was in front of Cathedral Square."

—Kevin Hannon, "In My Own Time," *Old Limerick Journal* 16

"A pretty tender sight it is in the midst of this filth and wretchedness to see the women and children together. It makes a sunshine in a dark place. . . ."

—**William Makepeace Thackeray,**
An Irish Scrapbook of 1842

The streets belonged to the children.

Old-fashioned candy store.

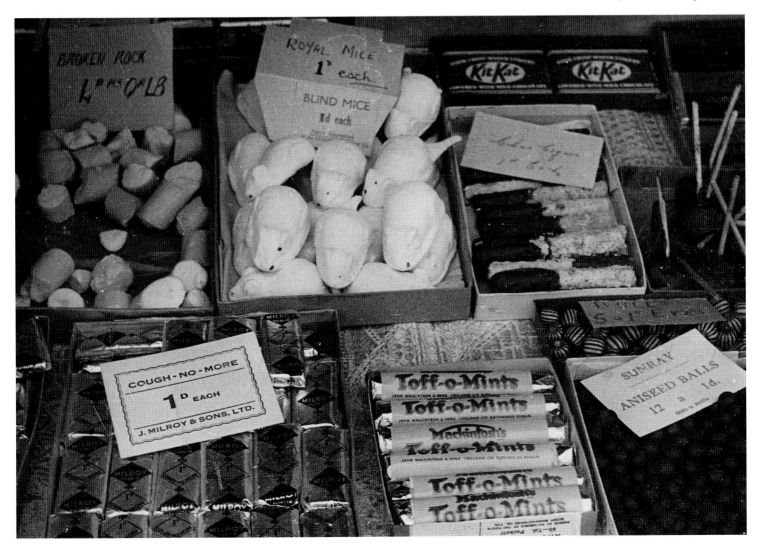

While some children raced around the streets, others, like the small girl below, went rather nervously to church.

"But we all retained one common goal in life and that was to leave school at fourteen years, get into long pants, find a job as a messenger boy on a bike and have a few bob to spend—after we had given the wages to our mothers."

—Paul Malone,
"Memories of Picquet Lane,"
Old Limerick Journal 16

Champion boy dancer W. Ryan, displaying his medals on an apron, around 1929. Mothers anxious to keep their children away from the streets might enroll them in the Irish folk-dancing fraternity.

School Days

There was nothing unusual in the punishment that Frank McCourt and his schoolmates endured at the hands of their teachers in Leamy's National School. Generations of Irish children were terrorized by the strap and the cane in the years before corporal punishment in schools was banned. Yet there were also exceptions: teachers who cared about whether their pupils had proper shoes or not; teachers who genuinely loved the subjects they taught. In the same way, there were priests who did not close their hearts and minds to the suffering around them. But it was not a time when tender-heartedness was encouraged. In his memoir of a childhood spent in the poorer quarters of Cork, the poet Patrick Galvin vividly recalls a beating he received for missing Sunday Mass (see opposite page).

Poor Irish schoolchildren receiving handouts of bread from a nun in the early years of the century.

Under the watchful eye of a lay
Brother teacher, schoolchildren
put on a brave face during the
visit of a not-very-merry
Santa Claus.

"Connors and I departed. We sank into Hell. The Devil was pushing red hot pokers into our ears and Brother Reynolds was beating us across the palms of the hands with a pure ash cane. Six slaps each and an extra one for Sunday because that was a holy day.

"My friend Connors thought holy days were a cod and said his mother had invented them for the sole purpose of torturing his father. When he told Brother Reynolds that, Brother Reynolds beat him again until the cane split wide open—and then he told him to kneel on the floor and ask God for forgiveness.

"He had three ash canes and he used them with zeal on the palms of those who had not been to ten o'clock mass. And when those canes were broken on the palms of children who were forever damned he'd send me down to the Institute of the Blind to collect more canes."

—**Patrick Galvin**,
Song for a Poor Boy

45

Life in the Neighborhood

Irish charladies.

Where government had nothing to offer, and charity was both insufficient and cold-hearted, the people at the bottom of the heap had to rely on one another. Areas like the Lanes of Limerick or the Liberties of Dublin were looked on with horror by people who lived elsewhere as the abodes of dirt and crime. Within these close-packed streets there was an enduring spirit of community and mutual help, despite all the frictions and hardships. Often there was little they could do, but simply a word, a gesture, or a cup of tea could help to maintain the self-respect of someone even worse-off.

A back-street scene of the 1940s.

"Hokey loaded four bags of coal on the ass and cart and pulled him on to the weighbridge. When he was weighed-out correctly, the ass would not move off the scales. Hokey pushed it, pulled it, lit matches under it, but still the ass refused to move. The sweat was pouring off Hokey as he came to the office window. He took off his cap to mop his brow, and then he said:

'Mr T., you're an intelligent man. Could you tell me something, Mr T.?'

I said to myself quickly, 'I hope he isn't going to ask me how to get the ass off the scales.'

'Mr T.,' said Hokey again. 'Can you ever tell me how in the name of God did Jesus Christ escape into Egypt on an ass?' "

—Eamonn MacThomáis,
The Labour and the Royal

Keeping an eye on the neighbors' children.

Washing day in the back courtyards.

The Emergency

In neutral Ireland, this was the name given to the period of World War II, 1939–1945. Despite pressure from Britain and, when it had declared war, from the United States, Ireland also maintained formal diplomatic relations with Germany and Japan. As in previous centuries, Irish volunteers fought both for Britain and for Britain's enemies; and many crossed the Irish Sea to England, to earn money in the war economy that could not be earned in Ireland. The flow of emigration of course came to a complete halt. Ireland suffered as a result of the German blockade of the British Isles, and there were shortages of every imported commodity. These were borne with typical wry humor and a tendency to blame the government.

"By the year 1942 . . . it was illegal to sell flour without a licence. As far as we knew there were no ships which were prepared to risk the mine-swept seas to bring us wheat. So the Government made an order that the millers were to get 100% flour from the wheat. The result was black or brown bread. . . .

"Bless them all, bless them all,
    The long and the short and the tall;
Bless de Valera and Sean McEntee
    For giving us the black bread and the half-ounce of tea.
But we're saying goodbye to them all,
    As back to the barracks we crawl,
If we don't get cocoa we're going to go loco,
    So cheer up, me lads, bless 'em all."

—Eamonn MacThomáis,
The Labour and The Royal

Stalwart members of the Irish army stand guard at Maryborough (now Portlaoise) railroad station in 1940.

Market day, 1940. Despite wartime shortages, life in the Irish Free State went on much as normal.

Censors, Confraternities, and Movie-goers

Ireland, still a "Free State" rather than a fully independent Republic (as it became in 1948), was a very new political entity, very conscious of its past history, and of the cultural influence of its powerful neighbor; its leaders were anxious to establish its own ethos as a nation state. The Church had played a great part in maintaining the national identity, and it now assumed the role of moral guardian to a young country. Movies, books, magazines and newspapers were all regularly and carefully vetted to ensure that nothing considered immoral by the censors should get through. This gave rise to many absurd situations, including the banning of such modern masterpieces of Irish writing as James Joyce's Ulysses, *as well as many less controversial works. British and American newspapers and magazines were often distributed with intriguing gaps where offending pages or articles had been removed.*

Younger people especially chafed against the restrictions of censorship, and it was with boys in mind that the Church set up bodies like the Confraternity, a vigorously evangelical roadshow which was especially strong in Limerick. The hope was that such spiritual missions to the youth of the country would encourage them away from less spiritual matters. Despite the enthusiasm with which the Confraternity was promoted, however, cinema-going flourished, and there was considerable undercover trade in "forbidden" books.

Cinema Days

If religion was the opium of the masses in the drab Ireland of the 1930s and 40s, then cinema was surely their champagne. The Catholic hierarchy railed against the influence of foreign films, claiming that they were a "danger to the faith and virtue of the young" and "openly anti-Catholic" (Doctor Magee, Bishop of Down and Connor, 1939). To Frank McCourt and countless thousands of other deprived Irish children, the movies provided a bridge of light across which they might temporarily escape from the miseries of their day-to-day existence.

"Any pocket money I had I spent at the local cinema. And when I hadn't any pocket money I stood outside the Savoy and Pavilion and gazed in wonder at portraits of the Hollywood stars. W. S. Hart riding the back lot range. William Boyd before he became Hopalong Cassidy. Paulette Goddard bathing in Ass's milk. Edward G. Robinson discovering a cure for the unmentionable. James Cagney in 'Public Enemy'. Mickey Rooney staging a Broadway Musical in his back garden. And most of all and most again—Ann Sheridan."

—**Patrick Galvin,**
Song for a Poor Boy

Saturday matinee time at the local cinema.

"The seats in the Lyric were long wooden benches like you would see in a park, but about five times the length. If there was a big crowd the usher would just shout, 'Move up there,' and push more kids into the seats. We were so tightly packed that, if you just got up to go to the toilet, you couldn't get back into your place.

So, many kids, rather than take a chance on losing their seats, would simply piddle on the floor just under their seats. About an hour into the show, a smell would rise up because of all the piddling done on the floor. And then the usher would come around with a disinfectant spray, and spray all of us, right over our heads—clothes, everything. I cannot remember anyone complaining, for usually we went out smelling better than when we went in."

—**Patrick Boland,**
Tales from a City Farmyard

You Have to Join the Confraternity

"It was, of course, the time of the great Redemptorist Confraternity with its hell-fire sermons and public processions. Limerick's boast that it had the greatest confraternity in the world was probably right, I never heard it questioned. The 'Fathers' (as the Redemptorists were better known) had an extraordinary influence over the people. They were dedicated workers and even the most sceptical [sic] could never doubt their sincerity. Some of the directors of the Confraternity had served for long stints as missionaries in the Philippine islands and did not shy away from the more daunting task in Limerick. They had the welfare of the people at heart, but they were victims of the times they lived in, just like the Confraternity men whom they conditioned to endure a refined form of mental torture."

—Kevin Hannon, "In My Own Time," *Old Limerick Journal* 16

The Redemptorist Church, St. Alphonsus, where Frank was enrolled in St. Finbar's Section of the Arch Confraternity. This inside view shows Confraternity banners.

Leave This Library at Once

"Purity by brown paper"—even a low-cut neckline was too much for the guardians of morality in Limerick in the 1940s.

The supervision experienced by the young Frank in the public library reflected the heavy-handed book censorship practiced in Ireland at the time. It was all right for a small boy to read in the library, as long as he stuck to the Lives of the Saints.

"Following complaints of the circulation of immoral books through the County Library, Clare County Library Committee made an Order that no newly-purchased books be put in circulation in the future until . . . approved by a responsible reader selected by the Committee. . . .

"Very Rev. Canon Meade, P.P., Kilrush . . . stated that parishioners complained to him of 'bad and immoral books got through the County Library,' and he added that a portion of a book which he had read was 'calculated to corrupt anybody who read it.'"

—*Limerick Chronicle,* 1944

The "Emergency" brought no new prosperity to Ireland. Men still went to the public library every day to look at the postings for the few jobs available.

"I can well remember the War ending in 1945, and we heard a new word, 'demob.' The men who'd been in the British Army came home with lots of money and we all had a great time. People got new suits and more bought radios and everyone seemed to be happy. But after a few weeks, the suits and the radios were pawned and that ended that."

—Paul Malone,
"Memories of Picquet Lane,"
Old Limerick Journal 16

A Century of Emigration

Ever since the Great Famine of 1845–49, emigration had been a major factor in Irish life. In the twentieth century the outward flow continued, abated only by the enforced intervals of two world wars. By the 1930s, the Irish people living outside of Ireland easily outnumbered the inhabitants of the island. For the majority of emigrants, the United States was the dream destination. Somehow, as the "next parish to the West" it had a closeness which belied the width of the Atlantic Ocean. And there were many vibrant Irish communities to help receive and settle newcomers. Despite that, emigration was still a dreadful wrench. Many would-be emigrants, like Malachy McCourt, Sr., and Angela McCourt, returned, preferring an uncertain future in their ancient homeland.

On both sides of the Atlantic there was a sense of loss and longing. Families and communities were broken up. Guilt and sadness were inseparable from all the partings. Many people in Old Ireland regarded the New World as a wicked place which was luring away their best and brightest. For many others, like Frank McCourt, America offered the only prospect of a break away from a life of poverty and hopeless aspiration. But he too, despite being Brooklyn-born, felt the terrible pangs of tearing himself away from what he knew, from the place which was home. In its charting of the young Frank's two voyages across the Atlantic, and its description of the life in between them, Angela's Ashes *draws the two shores of the great ocean closer to each other, and shows how, out of tragedy, triumph can still arise.*

"All during my life people kept going to America and there's not a family in this parish but has somebody living in the States. There was always a big night for anybody going away. Neily McColgan, the blind fiddler, would be sent for, and they would dance till day-clearing. Then, too, for anybody coming home there was always a bottle-drink; but these led to so much drinking that Fr. Fox put down the bottle drinks entirely. . . . Times at home were bad, and they all left home with nothing but the clothes on their backs. The old people said that good health and the grace of God were fortunes enough for any young man or woman."

—**Charles McGlinchy,**
The Last of the Name

Emigrants board a passenger liner at Cork, bound for "the next parish to the West."

New York in the 1940s—
Frontier of the Land of Promise

The towers of Manhattan seen from New York Harbor. For those who had left the U.S.A. in the Depression years, post-war America was a vibrant contrast. Once again the U.S.A. was a land of opportunity.

I Can Go Home Again

"Interviewers asked me repeatedly: 'Do you consider yourself Irish or American?' And I answered: 'Neither. I'm a New Yorker.' That's what I said before I returned to Limerick. Now I'm not so sure. For years I had struggled with the writing of *Angela's Ashes*. I had assumed the mantle of victim and blamed Limerick and everyone in it for my troubles. Twenty-five years ago the book would have been an indictment, an essay in savage indignation. Then the news began to filter across the ocean: all was not well in the city by the river. You'd tell people from other parts of Ireland you were from Limerick and they'd give you a pitying look. Americans, fresh from Dublin, would say how they passed through Limerick on the way to Shannon and they'd quote from a travel guide that 'the best view of Limerick is through the rear-view mirror' and, for some reason, you'd find yourself bristling. You'd want to say: 'Hold on, hold on. It isn't that bad. . . .' You'd want to tell the world: 'No, no. Dublin is worse.'

"While all this is going on you're wondering, 'What the hell do I care in the first place? I live in New York.'

"No, I don't understand that mysterious thing called sense of place. I don't understand why I trek all the way up to 42nd Street to buy the *Limerick Leader*. I don't understand why my brothers and I are so 'Limerick' when we get together, why we laugh and use a down and dirty Limerick accent."

—Frank McCourt, **"I Can Go Home Again,"**
from *The Irish Times*, **December 24, 1996**

"The freest spirit must have some birthplace, some *locus standi* from which to view the world and some innate passion by which to judge it. Modestly I say the same for my relationship with Limerick. It was there that I began to view the world and to develop the necessary passion by which to judge it. It was there indeed that I learnt the world, and I know that wherever I am it is still from Limerick that I look out and make my surmises."

—Kate O'Brien, *My Ireland*

Photocredits

The Publisher wishes to thank the following sources for supplying pictures for inclusion in this work. All reasonable efforts have been made to provide accurate credits and acknowledgements

Cork Examiner 2, 45, 58–9, 60–1; Dr. John Cullinane (private collection) 43R; Davison/Father Browne Collection 24–5, 37B; Mary Evans Picture Library 62; Film Institute of Ireland 16, 17, 18, 20–1, 55; Hulton Getty Collection 1, 10, 28T/B, 29; Irish National Archive 30; Limerick City Library 33; Limerick City Museum 12, 14, 15, 24T/B, 25 T/B, 26 T/B, 27, 32, 34, 35, 36, 37T, 56; Museum of the City of New York 8–9; Frank O'Connor 57; John Osman/Laurence O'Connor 7, 38, 46; RTE Picture Library/Neville Johnson Collection 39T/B, 40–1, 41, 42–3, 47, 48-9, 50–1, 52–3T/B; RTE Picture Library 31, 44
(T=top; B=bottom; R=right; L=left)

Books, journals, sources quoted in the text

The Publisher wishes to thank authors and publishers who have given permission for copyright material to appear in this volume.

The Old Limerick Journal passim:
Kevin Hannon 13, 33, 38, 56
Dorothy McCall 35
Paul Malone 27, 37, 42, 59

Patrick Boland, *Tales from a City Farmyard*, Dublin, 1990 55
Sir Charles Cameron, *How the Poor Live*, Dublin, 1904 20
Patrick Galvin, *Song for a Poor Boy*, Raven Arts Press, 1990 45, 54
Myles na Gopaleen, pseudonym of Brian O'Nolan, in *The Nationalist and Leinster Times* 36
Limerick Chronicle 57
Frank McCourt, *Angela's Ashes*, Scribner, New York, 1996 11, 25
Frank McCourt, in *The Irish Times*, December 24, 1996 63
Charles McGlinchy, *The Last of the Name*, Blackstaff Press, Belfast, 1986 61
Eamonn MacThomáis, *The 'Labour' and the 'Royal'*, Dublin, 1979 47, 53
H. V. Morton, *In Search of Ireland*, London, 1930 14
Kate O'Brien, *My Ireland*, Batsford, London, 1962 63
Frank O'Connor, *Irish Miles*, Macmillan, London, 1947 Photograph 57
Sián Ó Riordáin, trans. Patrick Crotty, *Modern Irish Poetry*, Blackstaff Press, Belfast, 1995 36
Society of St. Vincent de Paul, *The Saint Vincent de Paul Social Workers' Handbook*, 1942 18
William Makepeace Thackeray, *An Irish Scrapbook of 1842*, London, 1843 6, 12, 39
W. J. L., from *The Bottom Dog*, 1918 13
Richard d'Alton Williams 37
Women's National Health Association of Ireland 21

The compilers and the Publisher acknowledge the warm cooperation they received from individuals contacted in the preparation of this volume. Special thanks to Larry Walsh, curator of the Limerick City Museum and editor of *The Old Limerick Journal*, and Leni McCullough, of the RTE Picture Library, Dublin.

Further Reading

Patrick Beirne, *Mister*, Belfast, 1979
Christy Brown, *My Left Foot*, London, 1964
T. Brown, *Ireland: A Social and Cultural History 1922-79*, 2nd ed. London, 1984
J. T. Carroll, *Ireland in the War Years 1939-45*, Dublin, 1985
Paddy Crosbie, *Your Dinner's Poured Out*, Dublin 1983
Sharon Gwelch, *Nan: The Life of an Irish Travelling Woman*, London, 1986
Frank Hamilton, *The Changing Face of Limerick*, Limerick, 1976
Norman Jeffries & Anthony Camm (ed.), *An Irish Childhood*, London, 1985
Bill Kelly, *Me Darlin' Dublin's Dead and Gone*, Dublin, 1983
Edna O'Brien, *Mother Ireland*, London, 1976
Kate O'Brien, *Without My Cloak*, London, 1931
Michael Verdon (ed.), *Shawlies, Echo Boys, the Marsh and the Lanes: Old Cork Remembered*, Dublin, 1993

For hard-to-find books on Ireland, contact Irish Books and Media at 612-871-3505 (website www.irishbook.com/ibm.htm)